Where You *Love* Yourself

ALSO BY CATHY XINMAN

I Fall in Love with You

After the Door was Closed

Depression Will not Call You Back

A Secret Poetic Way to Love Yourself no Matter What Happens

Where You *Love* Yourself

Cathy Xinman

© Canadian North America Writers Press Inc.

Copyright ©2022 by Canadian North America Writers Press Inc.

All rights reserved, including the right to reproduce this book or portions thereof in any form whatsoever. For information, contact the publisher at: info@cnawriters.com.

Title: Where you love yourself
Name: Cathy Xinman, author.

Published by Canadian North America Writers Press Inc.

Library and Archives Canada
ISBN 978-1-7773970-1-2 (Paperback)
ISBN 978-1-7773970-0-5 (ebook)

For Night Beauty

You're simply the best, beloved

Where You Love Yourself

1- Cry Like a Child, Angry Like a Bird   1

  Taking Today to Begin the Process of Healing   3
  You Will Be Amazed by My Poetry   4
  Let the World Misunderstand Me   5
  Tell Him I am Faint with Love   6
  The Fragrance of Your Breath Like Apples   7
  I Have Set My Rainbow in the Clouds   8
  Place You Like a Seal Over My Heart   9
  Where Has Your Beloved Gone   10
  What If I Love You   11
  Love Is What You Are in My Heart   12
  I've Heard What the Maple Leaves Said to Me   13
  I Carry My Heart with You   14
  Everything Is Going to Be All Right   15
  No Love Lost   16
  Why Were the Old Days Better Than These?   17
  The Best Is Yet to Come   18
  You Will Come to Me as A Child   19
  Hope Is the Thing with Birds   20
  Is the Ground So Hungry?   22
  Singing Leaves of a Kid   23

2- Love Is Too Short, Forgetting Is Too Long   25

  Let the Enemies Take All My Sadness   27
  I Am a Desperate Person   29
  To Live Like a Poet   31

Let Me Forget You	33
I Am a Weak Person	35
I Choose to Let Sorrow Sleep	36
Let Love Not Help Me Sail	38
Let My Hand Touch the Knife on the Stone	40
I Have Put All the Tastes into My Mouth	42
If I Would Like to Be Rich	44
I Would Rather You Forget Who I Am	46
3- Man's Search for Meaning	**49**
We Are Also Longing to Move Forward	51
I Love the Pink of Perfection.	53
Man's Search for Meaning	55
Have No Readers, Not Even One	56
I Saw Dusk Passing by the Beach	57
Waiting for a Train to Take Me Afar	59
You Cried, and I Feel at Ease	61
As the Dust Is Singing Too	63
Crying for So Long, I'm Not a Poet Yet	64
4- The Love We Seek	**65**
There Is Only One Sun, Let Others Catch It	67
She Vowed to Live a Life of Luxury	69
Let's Feel Better, Look Better	70
A Love We Seek	72
I Am the Daughter of the King	74
We Will Make the Light of the World	76
5- Only One Day at a Time	**77**

I Feel the Power of Love	79
Not the Midsummer but You I Love	81
Greetings	82
Only One Day at a Time	83
Naked Eyes See the Unseen	84
The Earth Gets Dirty Easily	85
O You of Little Faith in Me	86
All Have to Learn to Dance	87
Hallelujah	88

6- Love Might Be Poignant — **89**

Happy Thanksgiving	91
While Snow Is Dancing	92
O Come Ye to Bethlehem	93
A Trip to Maya Tulum Archaeological Zones	94
I Want Peace	95
My Eyes Wait Reply	96
Vancouver Cherry Blossom	97
Come Slowly, Spring!	98
That I Did Always Love	99
Keep Smiling, Sweetheart!	100
And the Sun Says No	101
That Sun with Joy Is Bright	102
Dandelions - Nature's Great Healers	103

7- You Can Face Tomorrow — **105**

My Grapes Have Blossoms	107
A Conversation with Yourself, Thank You, Thank Yourself	108

Cathy Xinman

Breaking News
Angel Left Abby on Earth

By Xinman   October 30, 2020

Abby didn't expect to cry in front of Angel. It was Angel's voice that started to cry. Abby took Angel's hand and asked.

"When will you be back?"

"I probably won't be coming back."

Angel stood on the waves of the sea. Abby's tears were blown to Angel's mouth by the sea breeze, and Angel was lifted up by the sea. As the sea became more and more inclined, the wind screamed in Abby's ear. The sea invaded half of her body; she was almost dragged away by the waves.

"I'm going to fly to the high sky soon. Don't be sad, I've turned your tears into a poetry code, use it to accompany yourself. Humanity is about to face a catastrophe; you must prepare yourself."

The wind brought Angel's voice. Abby suddenly felt pain in the upper part of her right arm. She touched it with her left hand and found a blue transparent crystal ball the size of a blueberry embedded there.

But Abby quickly forgot about the pain in her arm, and she packed up each day. One day she came home in a panic, and after rinsing her body, she started to cough and feel cold. She lost her job, and her boyfriend left her for Asia. One night, her boyfriend texted her.

"I can't come back to you."

Abby held the painful poetry code on her arm, and the code seemed to look her up and said to her, "Do you think it will never happen?"

"He left me," she said. "He shouldn't have left me. I need him."

Where You Love Yourself

"What can I do now? The world has begun to isolate, and now there is a cataclysm of the earth's human beings, which is rare in a thousand years. How can you help me?"

"If you give me all the pain you are suffering, I will give you the code. You should use them to free your heart, to help humans and save their anxiety."

"No one's going to believe it," Abby said to herself. "Once again, Abby, you've got yourself a challenge."

No one believed Abby's poetry code, more people laughed at her poetic expression and looked down on her. She is lonely.

"I'm going to love myself and everybody," she told herself.

I was a person who couldn't go to work because of a cough. The whole world seemed to stop working. I looked at the sky every day, only the courier showed up in my neighbor's house. I imagined they must also need food for their soul. One day I showed a poem to a friend, and he said, "I need to be quiet to read."

I recommended it to another friend, and he said, "I need to read something like this to calm my mind."

A poem can change you, and I believed it when I waved with Abby at both ends of the road at the red light as I excitedly crossed the street.

"I don't think I had a strange dream. The fact is that after an angel gave me the poetry code, she flew away. When I woke up, the pain in my arm was still there, but I found out that it was also a pain in my heart." Abby showed me the red-skinned upper muscle of her right arm.

We hadn't seen each other for more than half a year, and it was as if we had just met each other. I said to Abby, "You are a sensitive and intelligent person, and your ability to change yourself needs to affect more people in need."

"Try to read some of my poems, take a test, and see if there is a change in your heart after reading. If your eyes are

Cathy Xinman

different, if there is a feeling of release, maybe you are a potential poet. You can change yourself with the abilities you have that you don't know before. You will love yourself in a simple way."

Abby said, "I can only give you these first. When sadness comes, you need to let it out."

"Fall leaves are fluttering, and it's time for me to start trying to change myself. When the beautiful season is about to leave, I feel even more lonely and depressed. And sadness makes my inspiration flow like water. I feel the gift of sunshine, air and water, the passing and cherishing of life."

"Yes, the falling leaves drift away; they have no sorrow. I have."

When the maple leaves are about to take off, where is the poetry code?

1

Cry Like a Child, Angry Like a Bird

Cathy Xinman

Taking Today to Begin the Process of Healing

Should I forget,
should you tell,
the birds, the trees, and the leaves.
Am I ready to forsake your golden hair
to the night, to the wall, to the mirror.

It's a voice passing by,
it's only the sound the room could bear,
it's the mirror opening the doors of its mouth,
speaking to me with gentle words.

O lovely, this is going to get real.
It's time to bring myself before the mirror,
and remain in it,
as it remains in me.
It's time to begin the process of healing,
Let's strip off our outer coats.

The mirror appears a shining wake,
instantly, I fall in love with you,
with my own image.
That's all I have to bring for today.

You Will Be Amazed by My Poetry

Mom, I really need
a pencil and a piece of paper.
> *Am I serious about writing poetry?*
> Yes, look at what the leaves say.
> Do I require any helmets or knee pads?
> No, do the leaves wear any protective clothing?

I promise you, Mom,
I will amaze you.

> *You will be falling down laughing*
> like the leaves down to the road,
> yet I have not called them.

Why aren't you going to wonder how the leaves are so majestical?
So elegantly, it landed right on my nose.
> My poem isn't any good,
> I swear to you,
> and cross my heart.

If you keep watching the leaves,

> *you will be astounded by my poetry.*

Cathy Xinman

Let the World Misunderstand Me

Leaves lying on the ground,
this is fall,
there's a chill in the air,
here is a bin to gather them all.

You were once up high in the tree,
the wind shook you off all the way,
the rain swept you all away,
this world seems not to care for you at all.

Did you love the world so much?
You gave your best elegant silence.

Will you be my darling angel?
Will you be my Valentine?
Will you marry me on a cold Winter Day?
Will the world misunderstand us?

Where You Love Yourself

Tell Him I am Faint with Love

The long, fallen leaves,
    such a great read aloud poem,
    for me to mind snowflakes

    that shouldn't be coming to the tree sooner.

I'll tell you
how you came into my heart.
Let us stay a little longer tonight,
no need to behold the grief, my beloved.

May you hear my murmur
by your verdant bed.
Your merry days never fall.
The rose so desired.
Please stare at me
for I am in the light of the sun.

May you reply
beside yourself with joy.

    When you hear me proclaim:
    You are my bridegroom tonight, today
    I have found my beloved.

Cathy Xinman

The Fragrance of Your Breath Like Apples

Awake, my darling, my leaves.
My beautiful one, see,
here I stand behind the tree.
I said to you,
nothing will ever shake you.

Winter wearing the sword.
All night long I looked for the one my heart loved.
I have prepared for the terrors of the darkness,
projected a path to victory.

Come away, my darling, my bride,
my beautiful one, see,
you have stolen my heart,
yet you ran away like a feather.
I have gone about the valley through its grass and rocks,
but did not find you.

How long will you hide your face from me?
My darling, my beautiful one.
Your tree is holding off its fruit now,
its fragrance as sweet as apples.

The fragrance of your breath right like apples.
People around the world, if you find my beloved,
please tell her,
no one will ever do her harm.

I Have Set My Rainbow in the Clouds

There is a little town
named Beautiful Rain Tower,
ragged and worn,
here stands a small tree
with a shirt that's torn.

Here is a little girl
in love with the autumn,
slick hair and sweet smell,
she is scared of taking a bath.

She is with a gentle prayer,
when the rain comes,
someone will wave and shout:
away from the tree and get on out.
My so dear leaves,
wear a fine shirt again after a bath.

Seven ate Nine,
rain is a very mean creature.

Noah, a man of soil,
planted a vineyard beside the tree,
drank some of its wine and became drunk,
laid uncovered inside the rainbow.
Who will remember the covenant
after the water became a flood to destroy life?

Cathy Xinman

Place You Like a Seal Over My Heart

You have become in my eyes,
my little tree,
your hues have grown,
trouble and distress have come upon you.
A cold winter day has sat down on you.

You are lying on my vineyard in a beautiful way.
I put my promise on you,
each is to bring to its fruit,
you are for peace and love.

But when we speak,
the world is for war,
its jealousy unyielding as a devil.
I have said thanks to the wind and rain.

Your sacrifice burns like blazing fire,
many water can not put out,
rivers can not sweep off.
You dwell in my garden with blessings.
May you hear my voice,
come along, my beloved
like a young stag.

Where Has Your Beloved Gone

You turned your hues from me,
they overwhelmed me.
My perfect one is unique.
Who has seen the one my heart loves?
Is there a ruddy fiction in the fall?
My heart sank at her departure.

There is the richest woman in the city,
her land is full of silver and gold,
no end to her treasures.
She has made a noise in the world.

My beloved is the poorest woman on earth,
yet she is radiant everyday.
Her head is like the purest gold.
Her hair is curling and red.
Her eyes are like the blue sea by the beach.
She made known to me the path of life.

Have you seen the one my heart loves?
My perfect one is unique.
She will fill me with joy once more.
My heart will be satisfied, and my tongue will rejoice.
There will be no more depression for those who are in distress.

Cathy Xinman

What If I Love You

Sitting at a table,
your smiling face is in my hands.
Oh, the place you will go,
where the golden things are.

Your curious stares are
like the lines of a poem.
I've never thought of myself as a poet.
Your poetry amazed me
that I feel the way to the sky, the unique blue.
To be alone,
I have come into myself,
explored for love, loss, and suffering.

I once cried for help
to the world, but no one answered — there was no one to save me.
Where do I go alone?
Beyond any wings,
and any of the pressure.

I loved you at first sight.
I sent tens of thousands of love letters.
You gave me the purest resting spot,
to me, to live what days are ahead,
to last, to sense the wings of myself.

Love Is What You Are in My Heart

This is a day
that you began to look out into the world.
A mom stared at the beautiful sky
which got dressed and walked by
as it felt like this little guy.

This is a day
that I smiled at you from the day and beyond.
I kissed your very first cry.
We started to love day and night.

This is a day
that I found myself praying for love.
May you have the desire of your heart.
May all your dreams come true.
May we shout for joy.
May your plans and wishes be granted.
May your mouth speak words of wisdom with the light of life.

Cathy Xinman

I've Heard What the Maple Leaves Said to Me

Your kiss on my eyes,
the beating of the trees,
the color in your body,
the power in your face,
they all made a way for me to be thankful.

Would it be ok if I opened my heart?
Would it be ok if I said that I love you so much?
Let's feel to be blind,
run to a hot beach.

Would it be ok if I felt so weak
with your disappearance from my view without a trace.
You might be invisible,
right in my eyes.

Truly I am looking for the Whiskey Jack, The Canada Jay, or the Songbird,
if anyone could see them going to Whistle, Vancouver Island or Rocky
    Mountains,
please let them sing songs of
my love, to you.

It seems that I'll
make you know
that until heaven and earth disappear,
you won't be alone by any means
until my love for you is fulfilled.

Where You Love Yourself

I Carry My Heart with You

I feel ashamed
for not giving you a raincoat, a sweater or a scarf,
before the ground is mucky and damp.
The paintings have been carelessly thrown,
like golden poetry all jammed on the sidewalk.
The beauty is to be crushed,
life seems to have no choice but to give in.

I am anxious.
You were sent out like a lamb among wolves,
brought before danger,
yet you are as innocent as doves.

Being a witness to my love,
you were ill-treated in one place,
take flight to another.
I love you in the dark,
you speak and act in the light.

My beloved, I am willing to be on your guard,
for those who kill your body
cannot kill your spirit.
Wherever you go
I carry my heart with you,
from dawn to dusk.

Cathy Xinman

Everything Is Going to Be All Right

When I am not at home in California with my cat Tiger and his daughter Kiki,
I can be found traveling around my house,
with my vineyard, beehives, and their friends, a flock of sheep.

I' m old, so are the golden leaves.
When we meet for an espresso,
we are sitting at a two-meter-long table,
one at each end.
What if the Obamacare doesn't work?
Trump refuses to accept loss.
One meteor doesn't light up the sky.
Please stay strong and watch your back.
I heard what the leaves said to me.

I enjoy my life.
In the morning I'm with my cats.
In the afternoon I sit down with you in the cozy warmth until the next morning.
Mostly I want to keep talking to you,
which is a safe space for us
to laugh, cry, and hug.
The face shield seems not to help protect myself,
but you let me feel alive through the pandemic.

I am making a great time to gaze at the stars tonight,
lighting a huge crackling fire,
so that you can see.
My heart is going on.

No Love Lost

Lost a unique sparkle,
the golden warm hue
shone in the sunlight.
My darling, the beautiful one,
I let you give all up,
leave to depart from me.

All I could find were empty spaces,
the old tree casts a shadow on the wall
in which I stand alone
and every word that I can't say.
I have put my poetry in your words,
faded onto your lips,
gone to the wind, to the river, to the sea.

I do not blame you,
your words are left untold.
Darling, *I love you.*
Surely my arms are not too short to hug
nor are my ears too dull to hear.
Only a refreshing cool breeze,
left me alone.
Winter starts today,
no love lost.

Cathy Xinman

Why Were the Old Days Better Than These?

In the interval of sorrows,
by a window looking down the tree,
there are no more leafy arms,
they were rained on,
it will be traveling places for snow.
My sad face might be good for your heart.

Instead, you asked me such questions:
Why were the old days better than these?
Why do you pay attention to every word people say?
You smiled at me when I didn't believe you.
The light of your face casts up.

I have found favor in your eyes,
accepted the words from your mouth.
Let us be on our way.
I'll accompany you,
head to where we can build a place,
set up an upstairs room and call it joy.

The Best Is Yet to Come

I said, here I am,
all day long, I have held out my hands to you,
seek you, ask you, come near you,
you stand before me,
I called but you did not answer.
My eyes are not seeing sleep day or night.

The former sound of laughter is not heard
nor it came to mind.
What goes under the sun or moon?
what I know is
more than anything,
it's about what comes from inside me.

Am I getting old?
You see, you know, but you don't understand
man's labor on earth.
As for you, you can be the best
that you can be at whatever age you are.

If I know
What is the difference between me and you?
Is that when you laugh, I will
sing out of the joy of my heart.
The best is yet to come.

Cathy Xinman

You Will Come to Me as a Child

All kinds of trees grow under the sky,
that are fine to the eyes,
yet not good for my mind.
Seasons grow and fall.
They never asked me to agree,
and say a tearful goodbye.

Leaves left the tear-soaked conversations
in the rain, in the wind
late at night.
They counted on the ground
that can't help but feel like it failed them.

I come, you go,
my dear,
without you I wouldn't be a leafy tree.
What is the fall without leaves falling?
What is the sky without your laughter?

Life in me is what you are in my mind.
You offered me, as to a child.
When will you come to me,
as a child too.

Hope Is the Thing with Birds

Today I finally know,
what I have is to begin with a bird,
like it's being whispered
in my ear,
it's being touched
in my eyes.
I speak of not having inhibitions, about being entirely myself
with a feather.

Today I finally know as an anger
standing outside where the sidewalk ends
fears of growing old and gray.
What I am,
nobody got how I was feeling.
Out, out.
Can I still rise?
Can I hug the fresh beauties?

You please tell,
since that poor swain that sighs for you.
I alone was born, given a lonely name.
Why do flowers change color?
Colors go, and colors come,
never before impressed.

Cathy Xinman

Can you please prove that
your lonely flight can change the sky,
cool face of the above
impressed even before.
Dear birds,
can you ask me for a kiss?
Can you give me a dream
with a feather.

Is the Ground So Hungry?

The breeze gently swaying
greens, browns, reds, and golds.
    Did I torment you all?
    Windblown leaves,
    why do you fade your face?
    So sincere.

Is the ground so hungry?
    You committed to feeding him.
    Will you consider giving something to him to drink?
    Why do you dry your body?
    So wistful.

Golden time and golden wonder
    as sweet as I could bear.
    Golden air seemed too much,
    your hardest hue to be calm.
    Only in one night.

Cathy Xinman

Singing Leaves of a Kid

What a golden day
to go out to play
with the golden leaves all the way.

I just saw a little girl
I never hoped to see one crying
my eyes noticed her opening mouth.

She told her mom
she brushed her teeth for two minutes,
but she only brushed for one
while leaves swaying outside.

I can tell you anyhow
I would rather see golden teeth than white ones.

What a golden day
to go out to see.
A little girl was bitten
by the golden leaves and golden bugs.
I brought the gold to my home.

2

Love Is Too Short, Forgetting Is Too Long

The rain took away the golden leaves, and autumn was about to leave soon. Abby was suddenly angry at her boyfriend's departure. She could only lie down in bed after she woke up every day and finished writing poems. Isolation became the theme of the world. She asked the poem code, "When can you make me happy? Are you the code of pain, or the code of happiness? Love is too short; forgetting is too long."

The code replied, "An easy way is to write yourself."

"Write!"

"Write!"

"Write!"

Let the Enemies Take All My Sadness

Take all my love,
all of me, truly, let it stop growing.
Stop wearing out and crying every night.
Let it not look like autumn leaves
that is full of life in the morning and faded at dusk.
Oh, all my love,
let the robber take it, take my outer coat.
Take a pure look.
Your voice is flying in the fallen leaves.
My eyes are faint in sorrow.
I was panicked by being attacked.
Your lips, that come closer, and your arms, that unfold,
Can't save the bird on the bed of tears.
Its silky golden voice is still singing,
to sing your name,
and this heavy world.
Let those abandoned souls
be reborn because of my love.
My love, let them sing in despair.

Where You Love Yourself

Take all my sadness,
all of me, surely.
Let it stop growing,
Stop tears from drifting cold nights and soaking skin.
Let it not be like Autumn leaves,
golden in the morning and broken into pieces at dusk.
Oh, all my sadness,
let the enemy take it, take the sounds of trees crying
and its tears.
I see man, in the air and wine, to be forgotten by this world.
No one island alone, no one,
can be reached by a heavy ship.
I see dusk struggling in the clay.
Oh, all my sadness.
Please don't blame me in the fire.
The world is tired; the exhausted bird has gone home.
I would rather suffer in vain, endure starvation
for writing the poetry of the far,
for singing the saddest love.

I Am a Desperate Person

I am a desperate person
to drive the suffering out of my heart,
throw the golden away,
and look out with weakness.
But now,
I wouldn't listen to you.
You haven't known my cruelty yet.
When you beat everything
take everything, full of everything
and was brought into God's promised land,
the storm is a jealous fellow,
it owns the greatest evil among man,
it separates the night,
smashes the air,
breaks things into pieces.
Now I just ask for one thing:
let me not see the fall
and the fallen leaves.
Let me not see you in the wind
and gaze at you in it.

Where You Love Yourself

Life is full of disappointment.
Don't let your voice touch me.
Let your tenderness be isolated from the world.
As for me, in the endless loneliness,
I only ask to be alive.
I am an insignificant person
to exchange dust daily for the sympathy of fallen leaves,
yell the touch of the fire with rain.
Say no more, my lonely mouth
the chest, split with a knife,
will no longer be afraid of darkness and suffering.
God hasn't promised plain sailing.
If my love for you is getting weaker,
that's because the wind is not strong enough,
yet you didn't open your eyes enough,
and spread your feathers to run on high,
and laugh at horses and riders.
You haven't made a fire on the cloud,
haven't generated your love into the sea.
And me, I haven't given birth to joy in the rain.

To Live Like a Poet

To live like a poet
I put myself in the dust every day,
in the flowers, grasses, and trees,
in sorrow and in grief.
Also put the sun in my heart when it rises
so that it will not go down.
Your departure brings upon great sadness,
causing songbirds to lose their fatigue.
The tangled loneliness
feels like a shadow gets closer and closer to me.
As joyful as the autumn,
gold spent lavishly without a care,
and left me alone
in the rain at night
to imagine I am lifting the sun,
spraying some splendid petals.
Let the sad soul reveal a new curtain.
The dust is perishable.
But here the light of missing you
will be everlasting.

Where You Love Yourself

I see new greens in the endless wind,
following me and my desire,
touching the deep marks on your forehead
and because I love you,
you tasted tears in your laughter,
danced to the cries of joy.
Leaves in the autumn will no longer fall.
I hoped rather than to love you anymore,
I would only love the ocean and sky,
the earth and mother,
the food and silence,
to love the birds flying by without a trace.
Yet I am different.
I cannot live without memories and wrinkles,
I cannot breathe without fragrance and without loving you.
I am to not make tire sadness,
making pink clouds go far away.
When the sun goes down over the sea,
you shouldn't be far away.
I should be in front of you.

Cathy Xinman

Let Me Forget You

Let me forget you
farther than the wind,
higher than the clouds.
Let me be lonely at night
and isolated during the day.
Let the tree hear my voice
through my silence.
Let you be happier than me.
Let the heavens rejoice
and let the earth be at peace.
Let the sea resound,
and all that is in it.

I look with favor when I am in silence,
love you in the dark,
love you in your departure.
The cloud feels free
while I hold afar.
What if you aren't in my dream,
it's the coldness that blocks the light.
Night locks me up,
as you are locked at the door of my heart.

Where You Love Yourself

Life is so lovely,
it gives me bread, milk, and chocolate,
and allows me to own the air, depression, and sweets.
Life is so rich,
it gives me the morning, air and sunshine,
and lets me enjoy smiles, sighs, and scars,
and make me not wake up crying.
As I am always in a dream
while life continues blazing.

I have nothing,
yet I am gifted day and night
with flowers, thoughts, and tears,
like a tree,
it receives golden, wild and weakness,
holding hope as well.
It's as if it would let you stay away.
I possess poverty,
and you possess the love I give you.

I Am a Weak Person

I am a weak person,
beholding the fields disappearing in front of my eyes.
The sky goes away from me,
the night is with its big eyes open,
the stars stare at each other.
I stood far away trembling with fear.

Dusk always comes as I feel helpless.
When I was blown in the air
with no wings.
No one would feel sad for me,
but that desperate heart would
still be looking for you.

The autumn is a tormented liar,
who lies with a tongue and boasts with its lips.
Gold is a lie that takes half of the night.
Let the wither of leaves hang on the tree.
What do I love you with?
You have gobbled up everything.

I can only be like the wilderness with nothing to do,
staying silent in anxiety,
hoping for time to pass happily at hands,
like a person without pursuit.
Don't place expectations on life,
I just want to love you while still alive.

I Choose to Let Sorrow Sleep

All my sadness
give you none.
I choose not to be the same kind as you are.
Immediately I am departing afar and flapping my wings.
I would rather the pond dry out,
and the dusk lost its color, absolutely.
All my sadness
render you none.
You're a false slave.
Lie is the blazing fire in summer.
It hits the sun and the clouds.
It overturns kindness and pureness.
It makes the autumn and gold burn.
I choose to have a kiss
of sealing you and letting you stay on the horizon.
I choose not to forgive you.
Although the fallen leaves are fluttering
to make heaven and earth gloomily,
I choose not to behold.
The world is filled with a face.
The ocean is covered by an oil painting.

Cathy Xinman

I choose to let sorrow sleep,
not to remember you in the morning,
not to look at you at night.
I choose to be ignored by the world.
Let love not to help me get up.
Your appearance is like a drop of tear,
that becomes a flood crest in front of my eyes.
I just want to climb up to the moon
and love you there.
Let love be in the sky, while you are in the world.
The earth is full of storms.
Your arrival catches collapse and autumn.
I choose to let the wind blow everything away.
All my sadness
give you none.
My voice is full of silence.
I won't let you hear a single word.
I choose sadness,
and you are beyond sadness.

Let Love Not Help Me Sail

How free I am,
as you are not present.
I may raise the glass poetically
to cheer for nobody,
to listen to naive voices and shake my head,
to sing no alternative song,
to look at the ignorant face and pretend to be profound,
to say silly words,
not to behold the dusk,
to present the twilights in front of you,
not to check your forehead
for whether it is full of dust and romance.
As the flame is like red maple leaf
to hang the wither on the top of branches.
The call of the bird is not enough to resist the vastness.
Ice and snow may not feel guilty for the freeze.
I wouldn't like to see the fallen leaves
that leave scars aloft in vain.
Beauty is struggling in self-harm.
The sky wouldn't like to be thin and pallid,
and me, I choose to flee.

Cathy Xinman

Let love not to help me sail.
Although I am skinny, I don't need to be robust,
I don't need you in the wind
to shout for me and cheer for me.
My body is safe and healthy.
Yet my soul is in the abyss.
I'm going to take refuge in darkness,
I implore you not to stop me.
I would like to write the saddest poem on the bottom of the ocean,
beseech you leave me alone and abandon me.
The evil men catch me, accuse me falsely, and threaten me.
I won't let them devour me.
I am not intending to wash my hands for indicating my innocence in deceit.
How desperate I am to live without you.
I implore you not to ignore me.
Let me leave those who speak friendly but harbor malice in their hearts.
Love, you are full of mightiness,
beseech you bring the flash of lightning
to tremble my heart.

Let My Hand Touch the Knife on the Stone

I must declare that I haven't known the darkness yet,
although it is in the most sinister night.
I still believe in love.
Even if the stars stupidly fall into a dark trap,
I still love the shining life.
I look up the shelter where love sojourns prudently,
that is the most noble solitude.

Oh, the autumn, that has left so much-
the tangled branches and raveled decaying leaves.
I believe that all the leaves will fall,
but not all of them have really lived.
I love floating in elegance.
Even if the wall is foolish
to lean on the wind in rain and at night,
I still love the shuddering banner.

Let my hand touch the knife on the stone.
Let the blood flow as smooth as life goes
as the roaring vulture fights in the sky
and climbs up the galaxy at midnight.
Life, that must go through dark ditches and deep valleys
to enter darkness and pain so that we may climb together.
Let the most beautiful scenery be born in the most perilous spot.

Cathy Xinman

Come on, if you do love me,
you ought to love my life,
to love my silent lips, that cry only for faith,
to love my sad eyes, that suffer only for strength,
to love the language that I speak in vain.
to love the volcano of my hope, that will erupt at any time.
I must declare frankly that I haven't known life yet,
but I do believe that life is bestowed by love.

I Have Put All the Tastes into My Mouth

When you have fallen asleep,
I'm waiting for the dawn
like waiting for a poem,
that springs forth from bread and milk,
to gain vainglory for my beautiful skin,
and trek in the darkness inside of me.
Let toxins quench sufficient sadness, tearing and despair.
The tears do purified things.
The soul is bidding farewell to the old bones.
Oh, it is the heroic moment in autumn.
What I really need is to lie down for awaiting,
not to care about the trembling of the skeleton.
I seem not to recognize it,
that is as a large ship in the sea
desperately crashes into an iceberg.
What I really need is to lie down for awaiting,
I don't concern about bullion
but only think of that life emerges out of the water.
Ah, I love the confidence that I have almost forfeited,
the waves have lifted you up, those are the spring flowers.

Cathy Xinman

When you have fallen asleep,
I am waiting for the light
like waiting for a song
to slip gently between my fingers.
I will no longer avoid the questioning of time
by asking me if I wasted the freeze of winter,
and if I let the sadness take enough cold air.
The land is doing uncovered things.
The pureness is to check who hasn't put down the baggage yet.
Ah, it is the most bitter moment of winter.
What I really need is to lie down for awaiting,
I don't care about the horror of the night,
and the sword of the day.
I have put all the tastes into my mouth,
and take the appearance that you look afar in the poem.
I endeavor to find Eva and leaves in the submerged Garden of Eden.
Ah, I love the confidence that I have almost forfeited,
the bottom of all oceans emerges out of water.
I adore this inseparable world.

If I Would Like to Be Rich

I am not intended to vent out
that I am dirt-poor.
Today a wise man asked me,
if I would like to be rich.
I replied:
although I am down and out,
I still have a blank paper
and a bald writing brush.
Although the root of tongue doesn't have sea,
my poem is like a surging tide.
Although it may offer kings to gluttonize,
I have the concern of the kings' indigestion.
This is not the way the superior man may be.

I like boring things-
I am painful for the leaves throughout the autumn,
but I don't have any concern for my beautiful skin.
Right now,
I am still immersed in my thoughts.
The reason that I may live is
because the satiation comes from my inner heart.
Gourmet food attracts my nose rather than my leaves.

Cathy Xinman

I am not intended to vent out
that I am dirt-poor.
Today a rich man asked me,
if I would like to affix bullion,
I replied:
although I am down and out,
I have a pair of jade hands
and a bottle of black ink.
My thoughts are like a spring well.
Although it may offer vassals
to write new poems while raising wine up,
I am afraid that the vassals are wrapped in flutes and pipes.
Although I may have no ambition in my bosom,
I am not a mediocre person.

I would like great things-
I have sung for the leaves throughout the autumn,
I salute every path
wave to every passerby.
Although the pandemic distracts the distance
rather than my leaves,
that treats me like a queen.
Sweetie, I am a servant who lives with my soul.

I Would Rather You Forget Who I Am

I would rather forget who you are.
Since heaven and earth are apart,
I have just discovered
that the night starts from my eyes-
the darkness gradually becomes clearer
ah, this is an accidental discovery-
at first, I thought it was you
who lighted up the night,
since those stars wouldn't accompany me to dream.
At first, I thought
that you have ignited the stars,
since the light let me observe the darkness.
This is an amazing discovery,
I must shake all the children awake
who are still in slumber at the speed of flame.
If the stars do not go into your dream,
That's because they have fallen into the darkness,
and the pitch-dark night can't make a pure dream.

Cathy Xinman

I would rather you forget who I am.
Since day and night are apart,
I have just discovered
that the day starts when I open my eyes,
the white light rushes into my face in an instant.
Ah, this is a sorrowful discovery-
at first, I thought that it was you
who brought the light,
when the sunshine pats the window
more and more intense,
as the water is boiling,
as the agony is blazing.
When youth embrace the flame with transparency,
when the awakening enters the world,
no one will be jealous of tears in life for resurrection.
When the light of joy illuminates you,
you are beyond the light.
I would rather you have a dream of deception,
so that the darkness may forget who you are.

3

Man's Search for Meaning

Wearing a mask, Abby approached the field. The players didn't need to wear a mask. The onlookers watched from a distance. Her heart began to flow like water. It turned out that the world was still moving, day and night.

Abby has been writing, she decided to remove toxic relationships from her life and her writing.

Let them go immediately.

She has stopped beating herself up.

She has decided to forgive herself for her past.

The past. Leave it there.

We Are Also Longing to Move Forward

As to me, a kid,
she has grown up by pulling pigweed,
I am not aware of that
If the pig has cultivated me or I have altered the pig,
It is said that a poem of mine is not worth its ration
I think it tells the truth.

Every day a skinny girl,
she doesn't have the plait tied with a piece of red yarn,
she doesn't have the shoes made of plastic material,
her long hair is graceful and free,
her toes are pure and spotless,
I am not aware of that if she faces to the dawn
or the dawn greets her.

Many trees have passed by her.
A lot of leaves have flown over her.
I am not certain of that
if the leaves of tree would like to love her
or she doesn't perceive love yet.

She carries a small pack basket
and the grass with river mud on her back.
I am not certain of that if nature brings her happiness
or she is still adorable with a basket.
Her speechless face is flushed.
The morning of green grass is refreshing,
that offers the most pristine food to the pig.

Where You Love Yourself

She also would like to turn the grass
that she pulls every day, into a poem,
and read to the pig.
The pig did tell the truth today.
The little girl felt rejection and contempt,
but she decided to continue to love pigs,
and resume to pull pigweed,

She invites me
to embrace the kind of love together.
Perhaps I may be confused, conflicted and fidgeted,
but we are more eager to move forward.

Cathy Xinman

I Love the Pink of Perfection.

It is real,
the poetry hasn't shaped up for today.
I have asked the leaves,
they don't have it either.
I have asked the lane,
it says that the poem has been given to me.
I have asked the soccer,
this guy, who emerges
but ignores me.

It is a hefty and prolonged winter-
Toronto is enshrouded by ice and snow,
Los Angeles, the city of Angels, has shut down its doors for guests.
Vancouver has enacted a social gathering ban one after another.
This is the winter that is persecuted by horror.
It is only you, soccer, that has endeavored roundly running.
I have recognized you from a distance,
but I can't catch up with you,
You ought to care about me.

I love perfection,
love billowing waves and green hills,
love the fall's moon, the spring breeze,
and the dusk that remains there.
I have seen the mist rising on the withered
amidst the vicissitudes and the full moon,
where my joy is pervading in the air.
I have seen the halo of full moon afar,
that is the brilliance of the sun.
Ah, this is a shift moment of time between the sun and the moon.

Where You Love Yourself

There are so many things in life that don't need to be chatted gaily.
I love puppies in thin clothes and waiting with me together.
He is excited and trembling slightly all over his body.
Oh, I love this still scene.
The car is rushing through,
I and puppy are awaiting,
as waves are waiting for heroes,
as a tree trunk is waiting for branches and leaves,
as the unstrained wines are waiting for reunion.

Cathy Xinman

Man's Search for Meaning

Meaning of this year
is to accumulate distance.
Worries of this year,
is to carry out naive things-
I collect autumn leaves
in my eyes, at night, in the bird's nest,
and wait for you under the tree.
My happiness is here.

Trees get closer, without sunlight,
they all like patients.
How can one love

someone as I am.

As I break the night sky,
the stars only fall into the water.
My sadness
let me watch, watch all day.

I can't prove that ants
It will take care of my anxiety.
I raise my endeavor
so that every tree can see.
Let those who can't cry
can also be in tears.
Let me listen, listen all day
as a mother.

Where You Love Yourself

Have No Readers, Not Even One

I see that everyone is a poet
who however never write poems,
none ever comes,
as they are cherishing life,
to pursue happiness in their own way.
So be silent
as I have no readers,
not even one
who would like to read, in the dark,
every star twisted for you.

Ah, you don't understand my stars,
yet I am still going to the universe,
to know those real verses,
to bump into those passionate love.
Let my love get sunburned.
The leaves on the ground,
cheer up.
Your weakness has fulfilled the earth.
My thought is hidden in the clay,
only you exposed the light of humanity.

Cathy Xinman

I Saw Dusk Passing by the Beach

Oh life,
in your language,
should I resume to eat today
or should the flesh
be cleaned up first.
Again, learn from fallen leaves for a while.
Again, linger around flying birds for a while.
Again, sit with the future for a while.
And then, ask you out on a date under a tree.
If you don't mind,
I would like to love you.

Oh life,
with your wisdom,
should I look at the thorns
on the eyes first
and stones in the body.
Should a woodpecker be called
to eat the bugs in my heart first.
Again, exchange greetings to virtue,
give thanks for the food.
Again, hold hands with the beloved,
and then, say that I love you softly.

Oh life,
now we are together.
I can see the blue sky
and see the ocean,
hear wind of winter, and the leaves of spring,
watch dusk passing by the beach,
watch the view of the back.
It is enough.

Cathy Xinman

Waiting for a Train to Take Me Afar

Today I just want to
care about nature,
breathe with half lung lobe.
Only the heart gets lucky,
its atriums are still there
and spread the trembling in all directions.

What am I waiting for?
Wait till sunset glow.
It's like love full of fantasy.
Afterglow kisses my cheek softly.
The wind comes whenever it likes.
The border where it left went out of sight.
The land is open, and the lane is busy.
All people drift in one direction.

Life is everywhere
and the panic is beyond distance.
The smile of a stranger may come unexpectedly,
that's more precious than ever.
Leaves and bark piled up on the ground.
A love grown in autumn
warmly
is addicted to the earth.

Yet the wind has come again,
it's more excited than spring,
more violent than a tsunami,
it keeps blowing westward,
it only takes a nap in the eastward.

Where You Love Yourself

> My loneliness grows in my mouth.
> Ears just want to cover it.
> What the eyes are waiting for -
> waiting for a train,
> taking me afar.

Cathy Xinman

You Cried, and I Feel at Ease

What alarm do I give you?
With tears of coffee?
Spit of bees?
Or the temper of chili?

Queen, my queen,
You are like a leaf
who now loves the earth,
loves lie and loves darkness.
Watching you fall,
falling into the warm water like a frog,
underneath it is a fire.
My beloved
I have seen danger.
What do you see?

I have cried all day.
You really deserve to be scolded,
really, to be beaten.
If you still can't enjoy
peace of mind.
If you still can't feel it yet
that I hurt more than you,
and more suffering.

Where You Love Yourself

>
> Ah life
> it requires to hear heartbreak,
> to see injuries,
> not only has no alternative
> but also needs more fire burns,
> more than fire.
> Ah beloved
> you shall burn and revive with me.

Cathy Xinman

As the Dust Is Singing Too

Darkness is singing in the sea
while I am singing on the ground.
We are all alive.
We all sleep restlessly.
What to sing?
To sing ourselves loudly.
Let's close the door.
The past has gone.
Tomorrow is not a reality.
Come along, my dear friend,
let's sing for today.

Singing for sunshine,
it is mine.
Singing for land,
it belongs to leaves.
Singing for distance,
it belongs to the sky and earth.
Singing for the appearance and heart,
as they all need warmth.
Singing for bits and pieces,
as the dust is singing too.
Singing for the sunshine
that illuminates all things.

Crying for So Long, I'm Not a Poet Yet

It's gone so far.
It's cried for so long.
The joy of standing.
The sorrow of lying down.
I'm not a poet yet.
These are not enough to write out the color of the cradle.

All I want is to watch in silence-
to look at the baby squinting and laughing,
to look at a huddle of the sea crying,
to look at autumn retaining a grim silence
for the birth of true verses.

I have found that mankind is fit for deception.
It's suitable for wearing clothes
while writing sunburnt skin.
It's suitable for drinking white liquor
while writing down heroes in all a piece.

And the street full of hangovers
is unworthy of challenges of any kind.
Moreover, life is full of holy power.
From humanity to personality,
from humanities to astronomy,
every age is always waiting for the real poet.

4

The Love We Seek

She decides to give herself permission to follow her heart.

Now she gives herself permission to achieve her dream. Then,

poetry code flows in the heart, in the blood. It is your child; you are its baby.

There Is Only One Sun, Let Others Catch It

I have never had a dream
or been on route.
I am not memorable.
Whether in good faith or malice,

I'm used to being invisible.

Whether it's one person or two people,
I don't even want to walk through the crowd.
I have only talked to the leaves throughout autumn,
and said solely in private.
When I can say nothing,
I would say God, for you.
Thoughts sometimes rush into the universe,
however, I don't expect to open the window casually,
as it's in my nature
to fear something new and alluring.
I am my own queen.
I can only talk to myself,
and revel in collecting words
that are like my children born in the chamber,
they are all unique and miraculous.
I wish nobody can see them,
they are private.
It's like my blood,
that only my queen can walk through.

Where You Love Yourself

My queen even rejected the audience.
One day someone said:
you will be like Louise Gluck
to get the greatest light.
Ha-ha, this is the sincerest placebo.
I cherish this voice,
it contains goodness and faith,
it surprised me.
For one,
the queen, who has never left the chamber,
will choose to accept some brilliant rays
that are through the darkness by adventure.
If there are a little more rays
and bit hot,
she would choose to squint.
As there is only one sun,
let someone else catch it.
There is only one queen,
let others forget it.
Ha-ha, this is a funny lie.
There are many great people
to be remembered or to be forgotten.
Yet what I have is my queen.
We love each other more than we love ourselves.

Cathy Xinman

She Vowed to Live a Life of Luxury

Being a queen is lonely,
being my own queen is quiet,
being an imaginative queen,
it is a kind of happiness.
She has no castle,
but she vowed to live a life of luxury.
She made up a territory,
describes fragility and despair,
praises love and bread.
Thanks to the lies
that let her identify,
it turns out that greed is the root of all evil.
She was carefully somewhat sorrowing,
gazed at another existence.

She began to make up realms of spirit,
and vowed to live a life without bread,
and fictionally made arts call her,
but refuses to cheat.
She must make every conversation,
every sense of affection,
come to penetrate and even stab the heart,
and lose the desire for bread,
lose the ability to survive,
only words left,
even if only pain is left,
she can't resist this kind of her own
beyond humanity
belongs to life but transcends the torment of life.

Let's Feel Better, Look Better

What do you do?
Tell the truth,
a rung on the ladder,
a cog in the wheel,
I am not good at
tasting such an innocuous query.
Surely, it seems like
a box to put me in.

I drink water,
yet I am still thirsty.
I eat food,
yet I am still hungry.
I write words sloppily onto
my bright surface.
What am I doing?

I am trying to scrape away
its cheap gold-plating.
Looking around to observe the world,
I am trying to find a series of lurking
under the earth and beneath the sky.

May I ask the world:
What will you do next?
Will you be every man's interviewer?
And ask me-
if I am still passionate about being alone for one year again.

Cathy Xinman

No ifs, ands, or buts.
I'll drink more water,
I'll sit down and eat,
I'll go to bed and wake up on time,
I'll dig below the surface
to redefine desires and purposes.
My dear friends,
let's feel better, look better.

Where You Love Yourself

A Love We Seek

Read spring with you,
read greens,
read you,
as if I read myself.
Let winter lose memory,
let the earth blow up pear blossoms,
let the wind feel cold,
and you feel beautiful.
Read time with you,
read the change,
read you.
It's like reading the soul.
Let the sadness lose its flicker,
let the stone sink to the bottom of the ocean,
the water feels heavy,
and you feel light.

A love we seek.
Let spring scenery pass easily,
to observe the rose,
after the snowflakes.
Our shadow is in the ten thousand green bushes.
Let the sunshine perceive.
You won't read that I'm getting old,
because time only passes by.
You must resign yourself to fate,
to read life with me,
read the youth,
read the journey, started by the spring breeze,
read its missing troubles,

you must admit defeat, as well locked in a seesaw struggle with the past.

When the glasses were laid on the table,
you ought to watch the Dayflower, and the wind grows leaves.
Stop arguing
whether it will rain or not,
or the rain will turn blue.
The air falls on us,
you must let it breathe.
In the gleam of grass green,
Let's not miss.
It's a quiet revelation.
And follow its teachings of the good.

Read spring with you,
read the sunrise,
it's like reading life.
Wherever we go,
it blooms.
Let the sadness turn a blind eye,
let love be unable to stop.
I signed an agreement with the wind in spring.
You will fall in love with every flower,
It's like falling in love with a sweet lip.
You will read spring in the green,
read the wind and rain in peace.

I Am the Daughter of the King

You are the king,
our eyes are beautiful,
my eyes are turning to you,
love is stirring in our faces,
spring is yearning for fruits in front of us.
Oh, you are the king,
You know everything about me.
Your powerful arms protect me from every side.
Your mighty hands wash away all my fears.

If I were to climb up to the mountain,
you would be there.
If I were to go down to the bottom of the ocean,
you would be there.
This proud world has hidden traps and nets.
As I walk, talk, or sleep,
you have rescued me.
Nobody can imagine all of this.

My soul is a desert,
but it will grow like strong plants,
it will be as lovely as a palace.
I am your daughter,
you are the king.
Let your wonderful kindness protect all people
who rushed to your side.

She decided to show love and kindness to others.

She has a beautiful feeling which comes from feeling needed.

We Will Make the Light of the World

Today I want to bless
foods, air and water.
Let you feel strong,
let you live a healthy long life,
let wonders reside in your heart,
As I will bless you,
and everyone.

Spring has blessed every artist.
I have created pieces of art.
My beloved, you need them.
Please behold,
and lift your hands on high.

This is an amazing moment.
You will cry shouts of joy.
You will hold me fast.
Open the eyes of your heart,
and lift it,
to feel the love that is in our midst.

We walk
forward with the blessed love.
We shall sing,
make the light of the world.
Let the light elevate every heart
and everyone.

5

Only One Day at a Time

She decided to find the dream locked away in the deep corners of her heart.

Cathy Xinman

I Feel the Power of Love

Winter got a bone
and wrote on it.
Spring got another bone
and wrote on it.
I saw bones dried out,
full of valleys.
I see spring
put breath in them,
wrap with muscles and skin.
I see life that comes back.

I feel the power of hope.

That will be my hope,
and be my love.
My beloved, you will see.
Spring says to the wind,
to bless every soul
with unending peace.
To bless every sad face,
like a king.
To make a path in the sea.
To make water flow in the desert,
like a bird flying in the sky.

Where You Love Yourself

These mighty powers,
these strong winds,
come from everywhere for everyone.
You will see
flowers and birds, love and hope,
will cover the earth,
like a baby
plays the sand on the beach.

Cathy Xinman

Not the Midsummer but You I Love

Ah, my lover dear,
your song makes the midsummer grow on the mountains.
I am a little lower than the sky.
Let me invite the deer,
the sheep and the cattle,
the birds and the fish.
Let them run to me,
I will let you win.
Do something, dear,
let your happiness be seen
on the mountains above.
Joyfulness is in you, my sweet dear.
Run through fire, I will for you.
It's not enough, it's not enough.

Let me invite a little flower,
let it heal your love's wound.
You'll stand on the mountains.
Let the petals clap their hands.
Let the hungry lions hide in the bushes.
You may hide your face too, my sweet dear.
Let them catch enemies
who tremble like giving birth.
The stars shall shine from afar.
My arms will embrace you at dusk.
Come and see something,
you sleep soundly.
Rest and breathe without a worry.
You think about my love.
Not the night dream, but you I love.

Where You Love Yourself

Greetings

All people greet you.
Give my greetings to men and women.
Greet Adam and Eve, who have worked so hard.
Greet the air and water,
who was on earth with me.

Greet success, my dear friend whose faith in my schooling,
Greet failures who serve anxiety.
Greet love and its family.
Greet hope.
Greet my dear friend weekend.
Greet Monday, who also is a relative of mine.

Greet stars in the darkness.
Greet rain and sunshine,
who work hard for the world.
Greet my dear friend faith
who also work hard for the world,
Greet myself, that special lady,
who has been like a lover to me.

Greet brothers and their sisters,
as well as everybody who is with them.
Greet fathers and father figures.
Greet mother and mother figures.
Greet everyone.
Please make up your mind
to know my heart,
as beautiful flowers are opening before you.

Only One Day at a Time

Before you, summer,
I wonder if you could speak.
I wake up early to observe the clouds.
The sky seems small.
Morning is something worn.

    It seems to me
    that I have a foolish heart,
    never so weary.
    Pardon me, summer,
    your legs are longer and quicker
    to run away.

You shall remain here.
To what, oh dear, shall I compare
a summer day.
My lips have kissed by your attractive eyes.
Only one day at a time, my dear.
Well, trust you!

Naked Eyes See the Unseen

Colors can still be seen
in a dark sky.
The light pollution and dust set the limit on the visibility.
The naked eye can still see fainter stars.

> Seasons are hard to determine-
> In autumn,
> The leaves don't change colors,
> nor will flowers blossom.
> In spring,
> faith gives the proof of what I cannot see.

Night grows still,
hope draws near.
What can be seen is that
your love is like the clear sky
to open the naked eye to the things unseen.

Cathy Xinman

The Earth Gets Dirty Easily

Once the sun sets
and darkness fills the air,
there is one hot potato,
that the sky drops.
It seems the earth gets dirty quickly.

Watching Star Trek or Star Wars is pretty neat.
An aerospace class castle appears to be livable.
A fresh new Tesla or Porsche Carrera doesn't seem to be reliable.

Fear does seem to be working with them.
If a virus wants a visit,
there is no need to email them in advance.

O You of Little Faith in Me

O me of little faith,
see maple leaves.
O There are little eyes,
see autumn.
I may believe in you.

O me of little faith,
stay on the surface.
Should I say yes?
To look down in tender love.
To look at things unseen.
Could the little leaves fear
when seasons are with them.

To see the waves,
To taste the wind in the rain.
O me of little faith,
see whose heart never sleeps.
Thank you to anyone
who watches the sky.

Who else sees other power,
leading the air.
Who else sees other beauty
offering to me.
O you of little faith in me.

Cathy Xinman

All Have to Learn to Dance

You'll love it, -
Walk, talk, laugh,
singing, raining, dancing.
O, look, sweet faces.
You'll fear no more,
sigh no more.
Winter is new.

If time has any new wrinkles,
then give them welcome,
then do not let your smile look ugly
nor your face as an angry man.
Your heart is the best.
Time is new.
Yesterday is new.

All kinds,
Actors will learn solos,
vocal warm-ups
and learn to dance from the show,
to dance with a group.
So gracious is the smile,
Gracious me!

Hallelujah

See the light to shine in the highest,
the day is born,
the sky is born,
the ocean is full,
the birds are flying.
A lot of children are born,
give them blessing,
fill them with happiness.
Hallelujah.

See the one who sends rain in spring.
See plants are growing anywhere.
Hear the voice over many waters.
The waters cover the sea.
The mystery has appeared.
O my soul!
Let me sing.
Hope has come.
All that I need is Emmanuel.
Hallelujah.

6

Love Might Be Poignant

She decided to reach out today to show love and help someone. She has learned a secret poetic way to love herself no matter what happens.

Happy Thanksgiving

As a day of giving thanks begins,
what can I use
to send Thanksgiving greetings
to you, my friends,
to you, my family.
How can I let you know
how much I appreciate you.

Little by little,
I got to know you.
Year after year,
you got to return
for the same recipes
for making the traditional
Thanksgiving dinner
full of love and plenty.

Love is the secret
behind the delicious foods.
Who can unlock the great fullness of love
that we have been blessed with.
Who is looking for Happy Thanksgiving messages?
They are still here.

While Snow Is Dancing

If you could cast your heart into the sky,
if you could see the hillside dance
alone
and the winds blow the coldest hair
into your face in frost,
snow is washing from the above to earth
in all its glory that you don't know.
It is pure luck that it could dance
naked
when you called
snow
like your images snowed in,
like the gifts wrapped in pure joy.

O Come Ye to Bethlehem

But you, O Bethlehem,
a small village,
hear the angels sing.
A king was born today.
There were shouts of joy and laughter,

O we found him
who was lying in the manger,
that was the crib.
A golden halo crowned him,
the baby, the little boy was born.

On Christmas Day.
O come ye to Bethlehem,
come over here.
What did we know about him?
Now, let me show you
a gift that's perfect
for all.

Where You Love Yourself

A Trip to Maya Tulum Archaeological Zones

Omicron revealed itself, snow came, Christmas arrived,
then all lights were sitting in the trees,
the city added a touch of glamor and excitement,
the dark sky was shining,
but the sun moved lower in my eyes.

I discovered the summer clothes
hiding from the sun.
The sun is shining
like a dog sleeping under a table on the beach.
How much I love
how quiet it is.
Shall we be saved from the cozy scene?

Riviera Maya is wandering around,
the spiny-tailed iguana answers,
that is a strange encounter.
In Cancun, Tulum ruins,
the iguana feed on leaves, fruit and flowers.
Shall we be isolated from a trip
to visit them.

It seems to me that everybody
is ready to take new photographs from traveling,
in the background, white sand, waves, the purest air, and the happy faces,
where questions of life are answered by the closest star.

I Want Peace

I want our home back.
If you can,
please help us.
Our brothers were killed,
our grandfathers survived.
I have no experience
to be a refugee.
I just need to be a human being,
I am not ready for any threat,
nuclear forces are not calling for peace.
I am a visibly exhausted person,
delivered last-minute plea for peace.
War would bring down the entire world.
Do Russians want war?
Millions are seeking safety.
I want peace,
I don't need a ride
to flee my own country.

My Eyes Wait Reply

My eyes wait for a reply.
Poor little girl.
Who is this spring?
Like birds,
come and look at me.

I hear his voice,
he says:
Spring is for you,
like ocean waves for wind.

The wind blows across my heart.
I give myself to him.
I must be coming in from the desert.

Wind, drive me!
Sea, take the desert!
Let us create a wave crest.

Cathy Xinman

Vancouver Cherry Blossom

How do trees respond to spring?
How do pink cherry blossoms
brave the cold rain.
They flower.
My poems are in flower-
flower of speech,
tiny petals emerge.
Come and look at the peak bloom,
they are set to reach.
Beautiful pink is blooming.

I'm not looking for breathtaking blossoms.
I'm not heading out for the finest blossoms.
The best of the best is in my heart
that produces flowers.
As the earth lifts spirits,
let us ignore the signs
of physical distancing.

Come Slowly, Spring!

I hear the voice,
it is knocking
and saying:
I am at your door.
This is spring's most beautiful song.

My young spring,
I love you!
Come slowly, my darling!
Let the faint perfume come through the window.

Let the perfume spread between my breasts.
Don't stare at me,
a young deer.
Let the flowers look like my smiles,
my smile is a rose.

Then, I hear the voice again:
Hurry up!
Take me to your home!
Come slowly!

That I Did Always Love

As I was on a way to the wind-
to the road-
I was wearing a hat.
I told my hat privately:
behold,
don't be handed over to the wind-
to the wild-
Their job is to spread the powers of the earth.

> *Let us take good care of each other,*
> *love will be our guide-*

I read a poem with a flower to my hat:
year after year,
love might be a poignant,
a bittersweet expression.
that I did always believe -
love will not cease,
love never falls.

Keep Smiling, Sweetheart!

Winter, spring, summer, and fall,
four seasons Vancouver enjoys.
It is likely to start with the traditional rain.
What will you bring for a new one?
Here!
Spring has officially sprung.
Mother Nature is repeating-
April showers,
May flowers,
once summer rolls around.
But us? Well,
what's the best thing to do?
keep smiling, Sweetheart!
Not for a warmer day ahead
but unsettled today with scattered showers.

Cathy Xinman

And the Sun Says No

Robert Frost says the world will end in fire,
or in ice.
Let him say why,
about the fire, about the ice.
Let me use metaphors in my poem
and come to tell him what was wrong.
You will love my readings to you:
The war against the virus will be won.
The war against crime will be won.
The war against ordinary people will be won -
he was inspired to become an accomplished writer
with endless ambitions,
with A Boy's Will.

Where You Love Yourself

That Sun with Joy Is Bright

The rabbit walks,
the egg walks,
the jellybean walks,
because he walks.
When you believe,
say yes.

Full blossom on the cherry trees sings,
the sun with joy sings,
because he rolled the stone away,
and walked on water-
when you believe,
say Easter Parade.

Dandelions - Nature's Great Healers

Dandelions welcome dandelions
that grow just about anywhere
that gently spread their joy,
the pure joy,
the maker of ability,
the maker of rapid growth,
the maker of reproduction.
Let them open up a bare spot quickly.

You become a leader of spring,
you become the best words
and send them to the world,
like wisdom books,
like Mother Earth healing.

>   *Bitter healing herbs*
>   *that reproduce its*
>   *seeds on the breeze.*

7

You Can Face Tomorrow

She walks through being herself, loving herself. Because of the love, the living love, she becomes the code of love, the code of poetry. As I love you, I can face tomorrow.

She attracted amazing people into her life when she wrote and learned to love herself.

Cathy Xinman

My Grapes Have Blossoms

When all fear is gone,
when the pruning cuts -
bleeding-
the sap exudes.

When honeybees find
the new shoot very much to their liking,

when greenish flower clusters-
bunches of tiny flowers-
do give rise with delight,
a buzz, buzzing
is excited about fruit set-
the stamens and the pistils,
the female and the male,
the delicate grape flowers are coming into bloom
from wind
from rain
from frosts
my grapes have blossomed.

A married couple asked me:
What to wear to a wine tasting?
Oh, vacation tips,
pleasing to the world
in the 'transition phase' of pandemic.

You will be filled with my joy.
Do you remember what I told you?
The true grapevine.

A Conversation with Yourself, Thank You, Thank Yourself

Loneliness, anxiety, suffering, release, love, peace, joy, hope walked in the heart of human beings.

As if you never saw darkness, fear and love, as if you had never loved yourself, as if life was in a swamp and sang in beauty.

A mission to survive, lonely so suddenly, she might regret telling you how to survive this way. She might like to keep her anxiety about life in a drawer like Emily Dickinson, as if she's never loved anyone, as if she's loved everyone, as if a woman's struggle against melancholy.

Let yourself inspire splendid words with intelligence.

Thank you for reading this book.
Hope you enjoyed it.
More of my work can be found at www.cathyxinman.com
Please feel free to write to me via cathy@cnawriters.com

About the Author

 Cathy Xinman is immersed in ink rhythm and agarwood and warms the years. Her works have been published since the late 1980s. As the founder of a multinational cultural and literary society, she continues to serve as a volunteer in many cultural communities. Known as a bilingual poet, most of her literary works take love as the eternal theme, deeply influenced by Neruda's poetic imagery.

www.ingramcontent.com/pod-product-compliance
Lightning Source LLC
Chambersburg PA
CBHW030041100526
44590CB00011B/286